Where Animals Live

The World of Mice

Words by
Virginia Harrison

Adapted from Robert Burton's
The Mouse in the Barn

Photographs by
Oxford Scientific Films

Gareth Stevens Publishing
Milwaukee

Contents

Mice Around the World 3

Living with People 6

Signs to Look For 7

The Mouse's Body 8

Movement 10

Senses 12

Food and Feeding 14

Setting Up Home 16

Social Life 18

Family Life 19

Cats and Other Enemies 22

Friends and Neighbors 24

Rats 26

Mice as Pests and Pets 28

Life in the Barn 30

Index and New Words About Mice 32

Note: The use of a capital letter for a mouse's name means that it is a *species* of mouse (for example, House Mouse). The use of a lower case, or small, letter means that it is a member of a larger *group* of mice.

Mice Around the World

Barns and other buildings are common homes for many kinds of animals. The buildings give them shelter and food, like this sack of grain.

The House Mouse is one of about 300 *species* of mice around the world. With rats, pigeons, and flies, mice are called *commensals* because they share our food and live in our buildings.

Some animals carry diseases and destroy our food, so we call them *pests* and we try to keep them out.

As farming spread across Asia and Europe, House Mice followed. First they ate crops in the fields and grain that was stored in barns and homes.

Cargoes of grain carried on ships accidentally *introduced* House Mice to North America and Australia.

Another mouse that eats crops and stored grain is this European Wood Mouse. It comes indoors only in winter.

The Deer Mouse of North America is another commensal mouse. It looks and acts very much like the Wood Mouse.

In Africa, the Spiny Mouse, with stiff, prickly fur, often steals grain and other food.

Living with People

Some House Mice move into buildings and stay there. They raise family after family, with none of them ever leaving.

Because they are surrounded by food, more and more mice live in barns until the farm becomes *infested* with them.

Coal mines and large cold storage rooms are other, strange places in which House Mice may live. In the cold storage rooms, the House Mice live in total darkness and they grow thick fur for warmth.

Signs to Look For

In addition to footprints, there are many ways to tell if mice are living in a building. You can see where they have walked by the trails left by their long dragging tails.

Crumbs or spilled grain indicate where they have eaten, but droppings are a sure sign that mice are around.

1315

The Mouse's Body

Mice are small *mammals* called rodents. Like this Wood Mouse, they have beady black eyes, round ears, and long, scaly tails.

Mice have two kinds of teeth. The long front teeth are called *incisors*. They have sharp edges used for gnawing nutshells and wood. The blunt back teeth are called cheek teeth. They are used for chewing food.

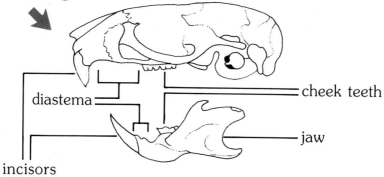

The gap between is called the *diastema*. It is important because the mouse can suck its cheeks into the gap and close off the mouth. This makes it easy to gnaw without swallowing pieces of nutshell or wood.

House Mice have grayish-brown fur on top and paler fur underneath. In warmer places, House Mice have longer tails to give off heat like a radiator, helping to keep the mice cool.

Wood Mice and Yellow-necked Mice are larger than House Mice. They have yellow on their *flanks*. Mice can sit on their hind legs to get a better view of things around them.

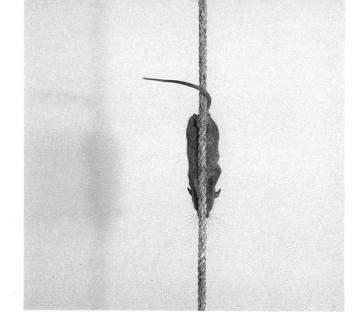

Movement

Mice have five clawed toes on each of their front and back feet. Their toes give mice a firm grip. Their tails also give them a strong hold while climbing and good balance while walking.

If a *predator* is chasing it, a mouse will race in zig-zags and leap in search of safety. The mouse's high jumps and swerving run make it difficult to catch.

Senses

Mice have four important sense organs. They have large eyes and ears, long whiskers, and a sensitive nose. They help mice look for food, detect danger, and find their way around.

Although mice have large, bulging eyes, they really can't see well. They can only detect movement. But their ears are very good at hearing tiny sounds and *ultrasonic* sounds that are too high pitched for us to hear.

The mouse's nose is very important. It can detect danger, food, and signals from other mice.

Mice have long whiskers that spread out like arms to warn them when they are going to bump into something.

Food and Feeding

Mice find a farmer's grain useful in winter when their natural food is hard to find. House Mice mainly eat plants such as seeds, nuts, and fruit. Mice often catch insects, too.

After they started to live in buildings, House Mice learned to eat many other things.

Mice eat any food that is left uncovered, and they will chew through wallpaper to eat the glue that holds it to the wall. This mouse is eating soap because it is rich in fats.

Mice can survive a long time without water, although they drink it when it is available. If they live outside, they find water with their natural foods of berries (above), caterpillars, and nuts.

In autumn, nuts, seeds, and fruit are ripe, and mice eat them in large amounts. They also put them away for the winter months in supplies called *hoards*.

These old shoes are filled with beans. The mouse will later come back to eat them!

9528

Setting Up Home

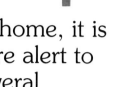

When a mouse decides to make a new home, it is at first very cautious. All of its senses are alert to signs of danger. The mouse makes several approaches before it is bold enough to begin to explore.

Once the mouse feels safe in its new home, it develops a network of paths. This mouse has made a nest where it rests and where its babies will be born.

The nest is made of soft material that the mouse chews into a hollow heap.

The mouse lives in its *home range*. It will stay there until it dies or until it is forced out by hunger or cold.

House Mice generally come out to eat during the night, not during the day. They are *nocturnal*.

Social life

As the number of mice in the barn increases, home ranges are marked off with each owner's scent. The home range becomes the male mouse's *territory*. If another mouse enters the territory, the owner will drive it out (above).

The scent of the territory-owning mouse should tell intruders to leave. If they don't leave, there may be a fight.

Some mice are not strong enough to defend a territory. They are often more scruffy and scarred than mice that do own territory.

Family life

Outdoor mice breed in the summer, when the weather is warm and the food is plentiful. Barn mice have enough food and warmth all year. Soon, the barn becomes too crowded with mice, and often many die or move to new homes.

Female mice can have *litters* of four to eight babies. This male is smelling the female to discover whether she is ready to mate.

The male mouse calls to his mate with ultrasonic squeaks. These are squeaks that are too high for humans to hear.

When the female mouse is *pregnant*, she becomes very aggressive. She attacks any mouse that comes too close.

The mother feeds the babies with her milk. The babies squeak if they get too cold or if they get hungry or lost. They are born pink all over.

When the babies are two weeks old, they have full coats of fur. They become very active, and begin to creep out of the nest.

The young mice leave the nest at the age of three weeks. They nibble at things they find, and they are soon *weaned* from their mother's milk. From then on they eat solid food.

Cats and Other Enemies

Most mice live short lives. They die from disease, cold, starvation, or enemies.

The mice in the fields are prey for foxes, badgers, and such *birds of prey* as this kestrel. →

The barn is a safer place for mice, but enemies live there, too. Owls, which *roost* and nest in the barn, and weasels and rats also catch and eat mice.

The main enemy of mice, the cat, also lives in the barn. It is often put there just to kill mice.

Because mice have no weapons against enemies, they stay alert for danger and run away when threatened.

Because they are inexperienced, mice are in the greatest danger when they have just left their mother's nest.

Friends and Neighbors

A few other animals share the barn with mice. Gray Squirrels may nest in the roof of a barn.

Mice also share their food with birds. Sparrows and pigeons eat spilled grain and nest in the roof.

These young Barn Owls watch mice from their nest above. When they are able to fly, they will catch and eat the mice.

Bats and rats are the only other mammals who regularly live in the barn. Bats hang upside down in the roof, waiting until dark to leave the barn.

In the summer, swallows nest in the barn, making a cup of mud and lining it with soft feathers. Swallows eat insects.

Rats

Rats look and act like mice, only they are much larger. They may live in the same barn, but the mice must be careful to avoid being eaten by a rat.

Like the House Mouse, the Black Rat and Brown
Rat came from Asia to Europe and North
America.

 The Brown Rat, also called the Common Rat, is a
major pest in many parts of the world.

The Black, or Roof, Rat (below) is rarely seen
outside of buildings. It spread bubonic plague,
called the Black Death, in Europe during the
Middle Ages. Both Black and Brown Rats carry
other serious diseases, such as rabies and typhus.

Mice as Pests and Pets

There are many reasons why mice are pests. More food is lost from mice spilling it than from eating it.

Also, mice nibble and tear at cloth and wood, looking for nesting material. In the barn, where there are many mice, the damage can be very expensive for the farmer.

Their dirty habits could spread disease, such as salmonella, a food poisoning.

People try to get rid of mice by setting traps.

It doesn't take a lot of mice to do serious damage. But if there is an infestation of mice or rats, the only way to get rid of them is with poison.

Mice can make good pets. *Albino* mice, with pure white fur and pink eyes, are the most common. Mice are tame and easy to care for.

Life in the Barn

Barns and other buildings are not a mouse's natural *habitat*. They are artificial. There is often just one kind of food available, and many animals find it hard to live around humans.

Here is a diagram showing the difference in the lives of mice living inside and outside the barn.

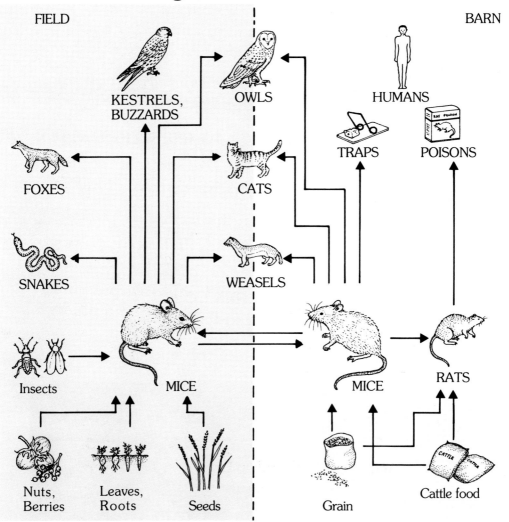

A barn and a field are very different places to live in. Mice in a barn are much safer from enemies, except humans; they have fewer kinds of food, but it is more plentiful and easier to get.

Unlike many other animals, the mouse finds it easy to live with humans. But this does not mean we must like **its** company!

Any animal will do well in a barn if it can adapt. The shelter, warmth, and food can support many animals. There will always be House Mice in barns, because when one is removed, another moves in. They are safer from enemies in the barn than in their natural habitat.

Index and New Words About Mice

These new words about mice appear in the text on the pages shown after each definition. Each new word first appears in the text in *italics*, just as it appears here.

albino ....an animal with pure white fur and pink eyes. **29**

bird of prey ...a bird that hunts and eats other animals. It is a kind of predator. **22**

commensals .animals that share the homes and food of other animals, including humans. **3, 5**

diastema ......the gap between the incisors and the cheek teeth. **9**

flanks ....the sides of an animal's body. **9**

habitat ....the kind of place where an animal lives. A barn is a habitat. So is a forest, a lake, and the seashore. **30, 31**

hoard ....a store, or supply, of food. **15**

home range ...the area that an animal lives in. It moves around this area when looking for food. **17, 18**

incisors ....long, sharp cutting teeth at the front of the mouth. **8**

infested ....filled with a large number of animals. **6, 29**

introduced ....when an animal has been taken to another place by humans. **4**

litter ....a family of baby animals born at the same time. **19**

mammals .....animals with hair or fur that feed their young on milk. Mice, cats, and humans are mammals. **8, 25**

nocturnal ......coming out at night. **17**

pest ....an animal which causes serious damage or spreads disease. **3, 27, 28**

predators ......animals that kill and eat other animals. **11**

pregnant ......of female mammals: carrying babies inside the mother's body before they are born. **20**

roost ....the place where a bird or a bat rests and sleeps. **22**

species ....a particular kind of animal or plant. The House Mouse is a particular species of mouse. **3**

territory ....an area that an animal defends against other animals. **18**

ultrasonics ...sounds that are so high-pitched humans cannot hear them. **13, 20**

weaned ....(of young animals) no longer feeding on their mother's milk; now eating solid food. **21**

Reading level analysis: SPACHE 3, FRY 3, FLESCH 92 (very easy), RAYGOR 3-4, FOG 5, SMOG 3

Library of Congress Cataloging-in-Publication Data

Virginia Harrison, 1966-
The world of mice.
(Where animals live)   Includes index.
Summary: Simple text and photographs depict mice feeding, breeding, and defending themselves in their natural habitats.
1. Mice--Juvenile literature. [1. Mice] I. Burton, Robert, 1941-   . II. Oxford Scientific Films. III. Title. IV. Series.
QL737.R638H37 1988   599.32'33   87-42609
ISBN 1-55532-334-0   ISBN 1-55532-309-X (lib. bdg.)

North American edition first published in 1988 by
Gareth Stevens, Inc.
7317 West Green Tree Road Milwaukee, WI 53223, USA

US edition, this format, copyright © 1988 by Belitha Press Ltd. Text copyright © 1988 by Gareth Stevens, Inc. All rights reserved. No part of this book may be reproduced in any form or by any means without permission in writing from Gareth Stevens, Inc.

First conceived, designed, and produced by Belitha Press Ltd., London, as **The Mouse in the Barn**, with an original text copyright by Oxford Scientific Films. Format copyright by Belitha Press Ltd.

Typeset in Milwaukee by Web Tech, Inc. Printed in Hong Kong by South China Printing Co.
Series Editor: Mark J. Sachner. Art Director: Treld Bicknell. Design: Naomi Games.
Cover Design: Gary Moseley. Line Drawings: Lorna Turpin. Scientific Consultant: Gwynne Vevers.

The publishers wish to thank the following for permission to reproduce copyright photographs:
Oxford Scientific Films Ltd. for front cover (John Beach Rodger Jackman); p. 6 below and back cover (Colin Milkins; title page and pp. 2, 3, 6 above, 7, 9, 12 both, 13, 14 both, 15 above, 16 all, 17, 19, 20, 21 both, 28 below, 29 below, and 31 (John Beach Rodger Jackman); pp. 4 and 23, G.I. Bernard; p. 5 above (Breck P. Kent); pp. 8, 10 below, 24 right, and 26 (Press-Tige Pictures); pp. 10 above, 18, 22, 28 above, and 29 above (David Thompson); p. 15 below (Robert Burton); p. 24 left (Stephen Mills); p. 25 (Bruce A. Macdonald); p. 27 (Robin Redfern); Bruce Coleman Ltd. for p. 5 below (Jane Burton); p. 11 (Kim Taylor).

1 2 3 4 5 6 7 8 9 93 92 91 90 89 88